CATALOG
Engagement Rings JEWELS

Por zoara joyas

EDITORIAL aMazon
Título del Libro: zoara joyas

Copyright © 2016 por zoara joyas
Todos los Derechos Reservados.

Edición: zoara joyas
Diseño de Portada: zoara joyas
Maquetado: zoara joyas

Publicado en (tu país) por Editorial Equis
ISBN-13:9781530444571

http://www.TuSitioWeb.com
Facebook: https://www.facebook.com/telotraigodesdeisrael/?pnref=lhc
Twitter: @benyojanan

Índice

Dedicatoria

In Zoara we offer a wide range of wedding bands for women, from embedded diamond eternity bands for wedding rings plain gold. Our wedding curved wings are good choices for women who want to take both her wedding ring and engagement ring on the same finger. The curve allows it to fit comfortably under almost any solitaire engagement ring diamond. We also sell wedding rings game of men and women for those couples who prefer to share the same ring style.

Whether you prefer plain banded, precious-set stones, big, small, elegant, platinum or gold wedding rings, Engagement Rings, you have it all! We invite you to browse the collection of exquisite wedding rings Engagement Rings at your leisure.

Prefacio

For some, their engagement day or period of engagement, whether it be two months or a year, represents the

most memorable time of their lives. It truly is an exciting time, filled with surprises, decisions and plans. For

Zoara, engagement is actually an opportunity to educate our valued customers. We invite those who are

interested in investing in a diamond engagement ring, but who are unsure about how to go about choosing

one, to visit our Diamond Learning Center pages. There you'll find a plethora of information, from

explanations about the classic 4Cs to learning how to decipher a Diamond Grading Report.

At Zoara, engagement jewelry is not limited to the classic solitaire diamond ring so commonly associated

with engagements and marriage. Rather, we strive to bring the classic to the modern, to find a balance and

place for those who might be looking for something a little more unique. Whether it be a Pear-Shaped

Diamond with a side stone setting or a pave set Princess Cut, Zoara is here to help you work within your

budget to find your perfect Inexpensive Engagement Ring.

We are also proud to offer you an interactive, user-friendly system to help you Design Your Own Ring. If you

don't find the Preset Engagement Ring of your dreams with us, you'll be able to create it yourself with the

design your own option. Nearly anything is possible.

Within our engagement jewelry collection you'll also find both women's and men's engagement Bands.

Zoara's jewelry designers have assembled an eclectic selection of men's and women's Wedding Rings and

Engagement Rings to suit all tastes. From classic yellow gold to diamond-studded platinum bands and twotoned

matching sets, browse our collection on your own or together with your fiance. The big day is coming

up, and Zoara is ready to help you find the perfect wedding bands for one of the most important days of your

life.

To learn more about how you can buy your very own Affordable Engagement Ring and How Much to Spend

on Engagement Rings please feel free to visit our jewelry learning center pages and learn all about

Engagement Rings Financing and other related topics on shopping for an engagement ring.

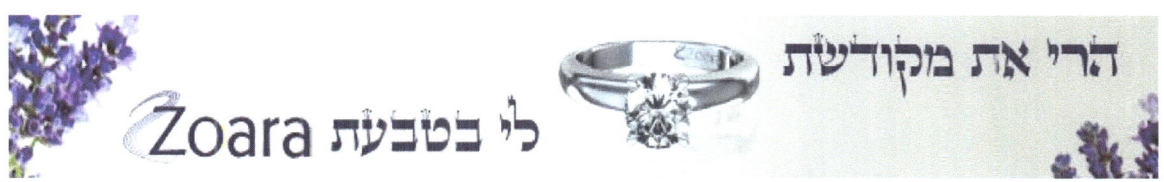

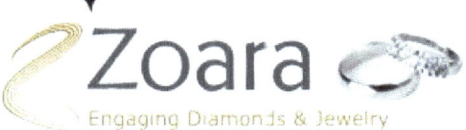

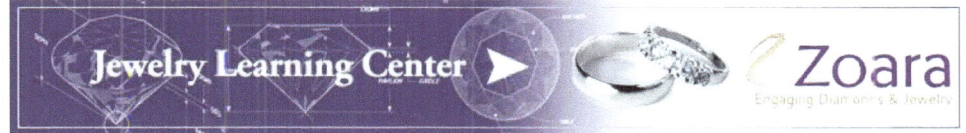

Engagement

For some, their engagement day or period of engagement, whether it be two months or a year, represents the most memorable time of their lives. It truly is an exciting time, filled with surprises, decisions and plans. For Zoara, engagement is actually an opportunity to educate our valued customers. We invite those who are interested in investing in a diamond engagement ring, but who are unsure about how to go about choosing one, to visit our Diamond Learning Center pages. There you'll find a plethora of information, from explanations about the classic 4Cs to learning how to decipher a Diamond Grading Report.

At Zoara, engagement jewelry is not limited to the classic solitaire diamond ring so commonly associated with engagements and marriage. Rather, we strive to bring the classic to the modern, to find a balance and place for those who might be looking for something a little more unique. Whether it be a Pear-Shaped Diamond with a side stone setting or a pave set Princess Cut, Zoara is here to help you work within your budget to find your perfect Inexpensive Engagement Ring.

We are also proud to offer you an interactive, user-friendly system to help you Design Your Own Ring. If you don't find the Preset Engagement Ring of your dreams with us, you'll be able to create it yourself with the design your own option. Nearly anything is possible.

Within our engagement jewelry collection you'll also find both women's and men's engagement Bands. Zoara's jewelry designers have assembled an eclectic selection of men's and women's Wedding Rings and Engagement Rings to suit all tastes. From classic yellow gold to diamond-studded platinum bands and two-toned matching sets, browse our collection on your own or together with your fiance. The big day is coming up, and Zoara is ready to help you find the perfect wedding bands for one of the most important days of your life.

To learn more about how you can buy your very own Affordable Engagement Ring and How Much to Spend on Engagement Rings please feel free to visit our jewelry learning center pages and learn all about Engagement Rings Financing and other related topics on shopping for an engagement ring.

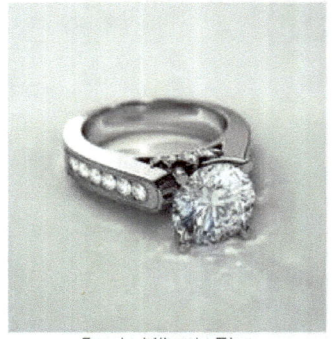

Ornate Milgrain Ring
Starting from $2,350

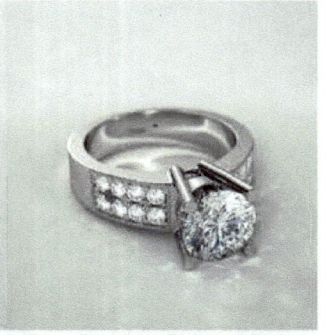

Pave Sidestone Diamond Ring
Starting from $1,880

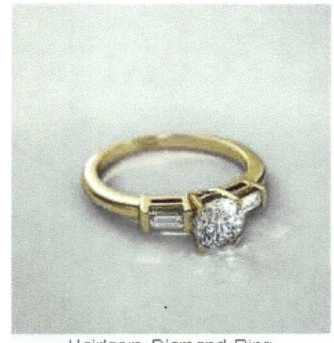

Heirloom Diamond Ring
Starting from $1,100

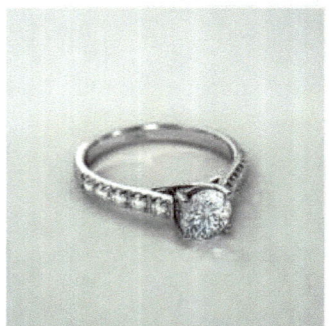

Round Brilliant Shared Prong Set
Diamond Ring
Starting from $1,220

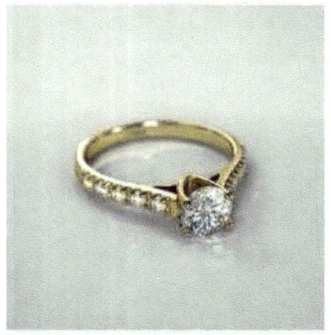

Shared Prong Accented Ring
Starting from $1,200

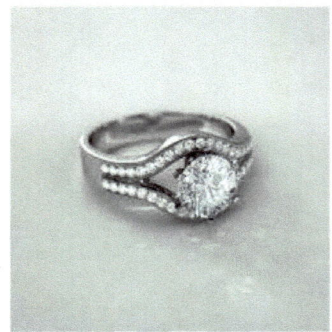

Pave Set Split Diamond Ring
Starting from $2,930

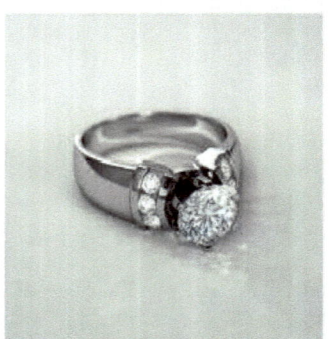

Channel Set Diamond Ring
Starting from $1,810

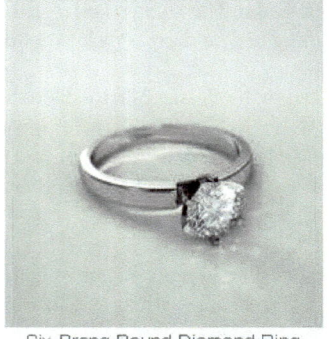

Six Prong Round Diamond Ring
Starting from $905

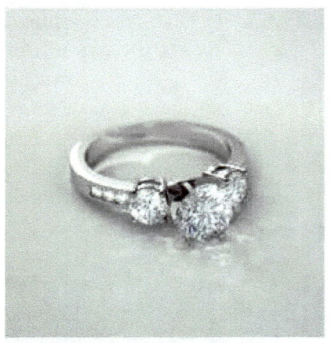

Majestic Engagement Ring
Starting from $2,490

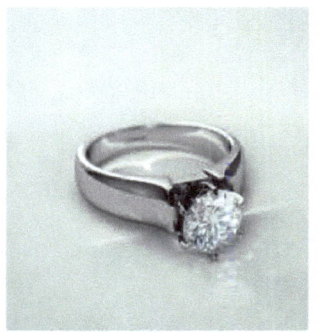

Traditional Diamond Ring
Starting from $1,100

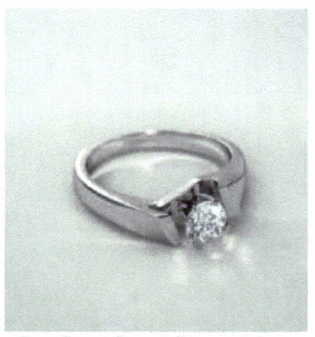

Four Prong Round Diamond Ring
Starting from $850

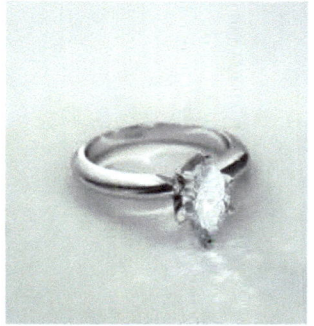

Six Prong Oval Cut Ring
Starting from $530

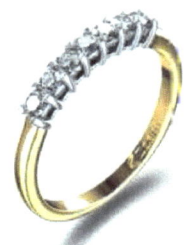

Classic Shared Prong 1/4 ctw
Diamond Ring
Starting from $775

Tapered Engagement Ring
Starting from $770

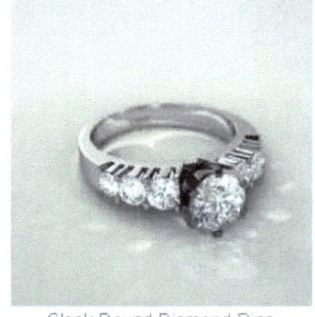

Sleek Round Diamond Ring
Starting from $2,220

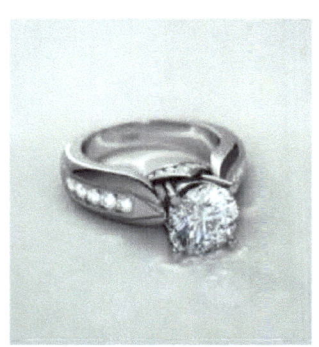

Milgrain Arabesque Ring
Starting from $2,180

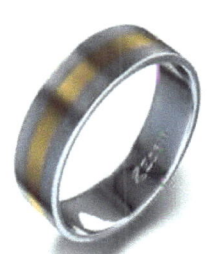

Two Tone Inlay Wedding Band
Starting from $720

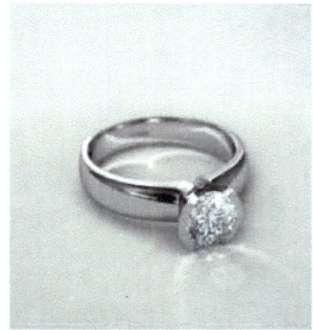

Half Bezel Diamond Ring
Starting from $860

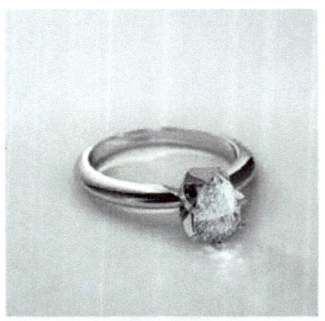

Pear Shaped Diamond Ring
Starting from $675

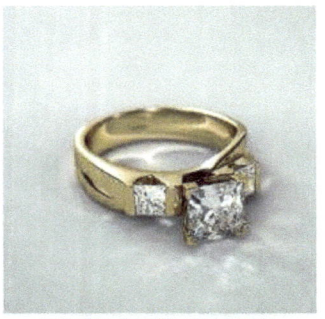

Princess Cut Diamond Ring
Starting from $1,600

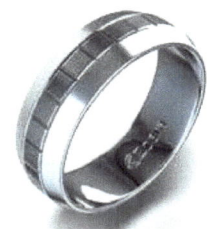

Square Facet Wedding Band
Starting from $615

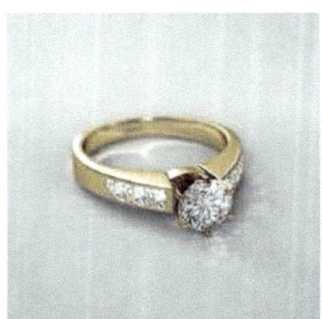

Round Brilliant Diamond Ring
Starting from $1,500

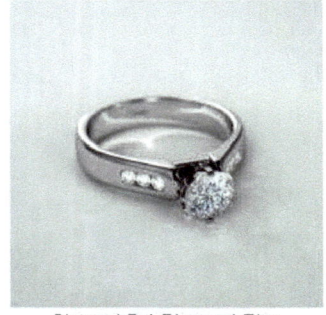

Channel Set Diamond Ring
Starting from $1,480

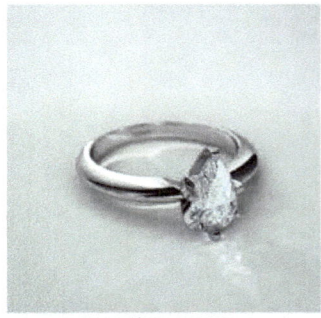

Pear Diamond Ring
Starting from $540

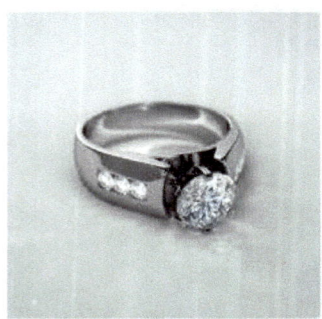

Round Channel Diamond Ring
Starting from $1,350

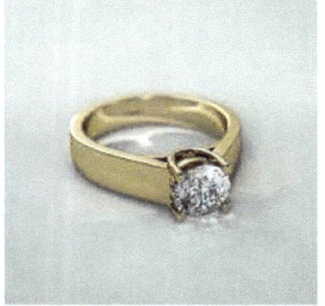

Four Prong Round Cut Diamond
Ring
Starting from $875

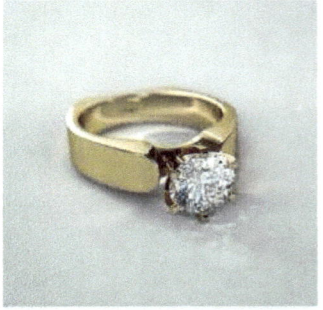

Contour Round Diamond Ring
Starting from $1,130

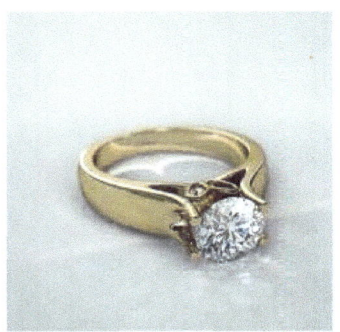

Side Accented Diamond Ring
Starting from $845

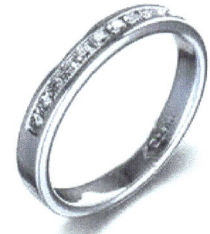

1/4 ctw Channel Set Diamond Ring
Starting from $850

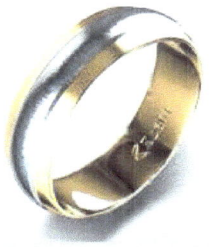

Step Edge Wedding Band
Starting from $515

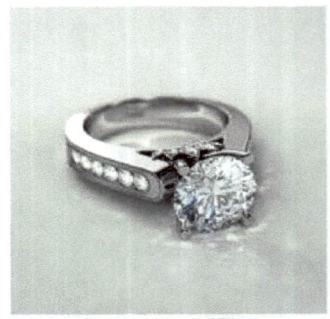

Ornate Milgrain Ring
Starting from $2,350

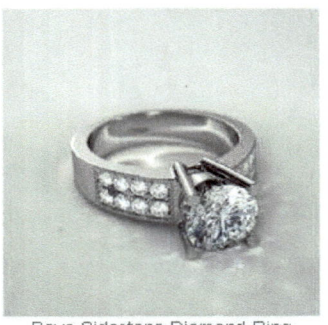

Pave Sidestone Diamond Ring
Starting from $1,880

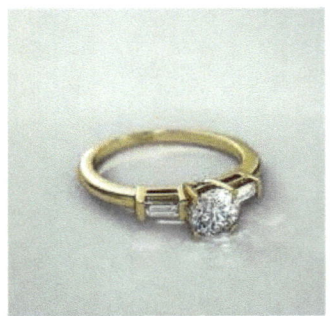

Heirloom Diamond Ring
Starting from $1,100

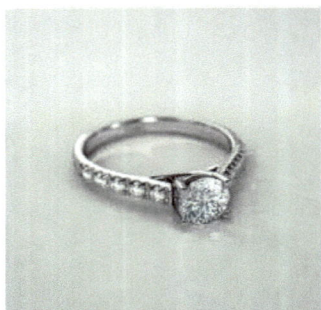

Round Brilliant Shared Prong Set
Diamond Ring
Starting from $1,220

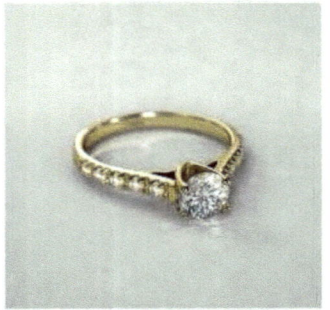

Shared Prong Accented Ring
Starting from $1,200

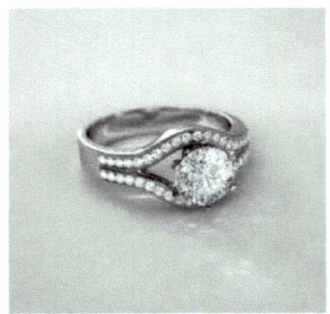

Pave Set Split Diamond Ring
Starting from $2,930

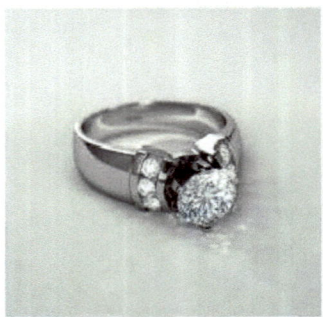

Channel Set Diamond Ring
Starting from $1,810

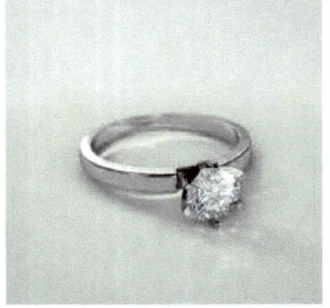

Six Prong Round Diamond Ring
Starting from $905

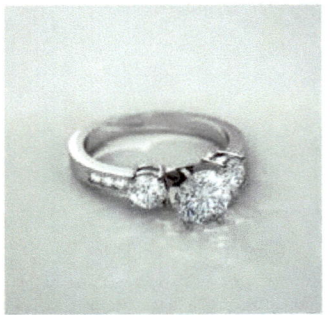

Majestic Engagement Ring
Starting from $2,490

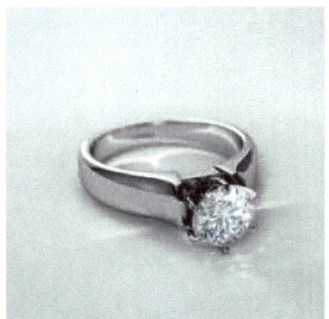

Traditional Diamond Ring
Starting from $1,100

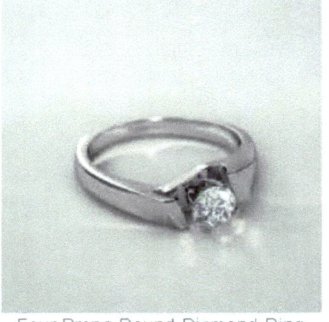

Four Prong Round Diamond Ring
Starting from $850

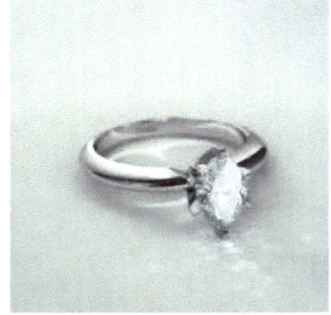

Six Prong Oval Cut Ring
Starting from $530

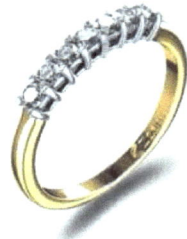

Classic Shared Prong 1/4 ctw
Diamond Ring
Starting from $775

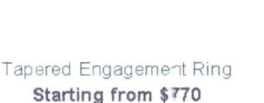

Tapered Engagement Ring
Starting from $770

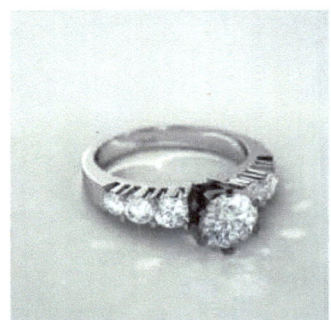

Sleek Round Diamond Ring
Starting from $2,220

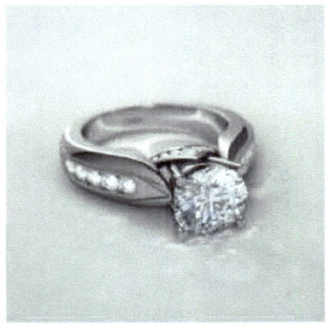

Milgrain Arabesque Ring
Starting from $2,180

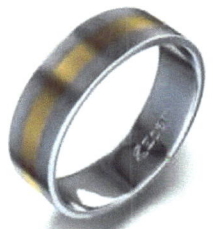

Two Tone Inlay Wedding Band
Starting from $720

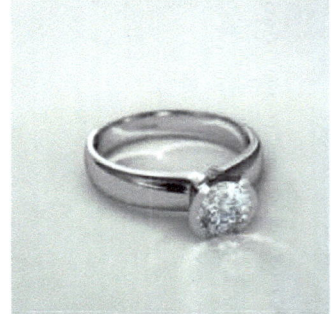

Half Bezel Diamond Ring
Starting from $860

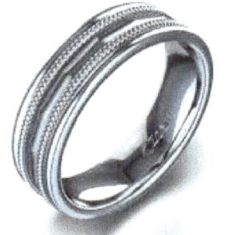

Faceted Milgrain Wedding Band
Starting from $595

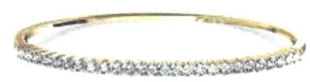

Dashing 1 1/4 ctw Diamond Bangle
Starting from $2,150

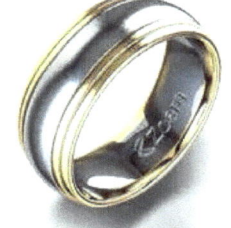

Brushed Double Ridged Wedding Band
Starting from $830

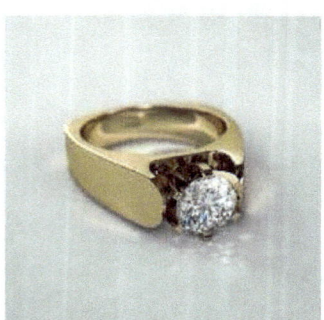

Classic Engagement Ring
Starting from $1,160

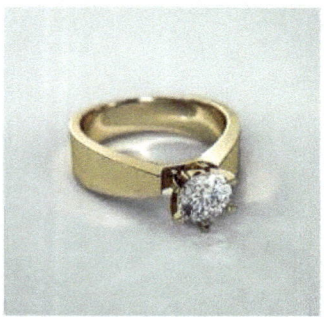

Tapered Diamond Ring
Starting from $1,160

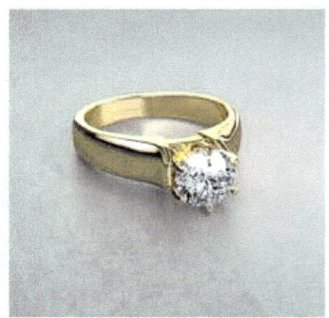

Contour Set Diamond Ring
Starting from $1,100

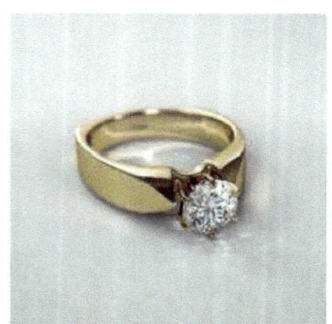

Soft-Tipped Solitaire Diamond Ring
Starting from $1,100

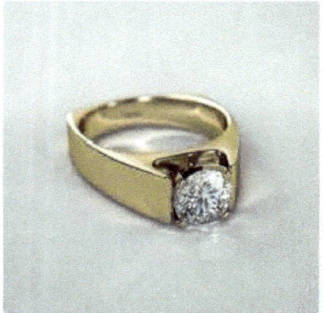

Sleek Tapered Diamond Ring
Starting from $1,320

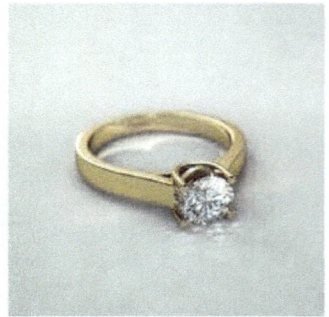

Arched Prong Diamond Ring
Starting from $910

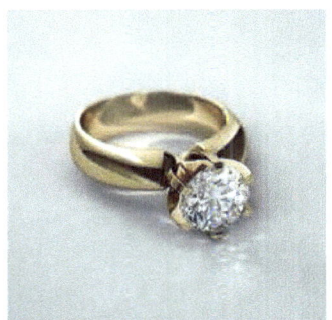

Tapered Shank Diamond Ring
Starting from $1,090

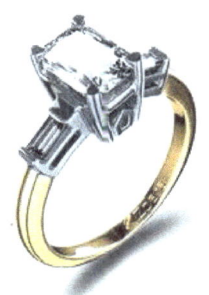

Two Tone Emerald Heirloom
Diamond Ring
Starting from $1,120

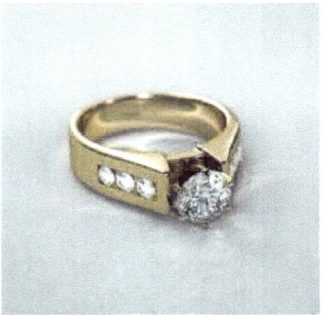

Round Cut Side Stone Ring
Starting from $1,780

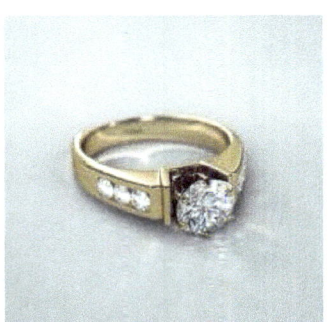

Round Cut Channel Set Ring
Starting from $1,610

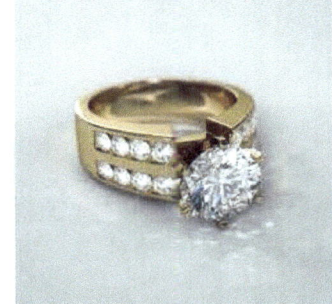

Glamorous Sidestone Ring
Starting from $3,070

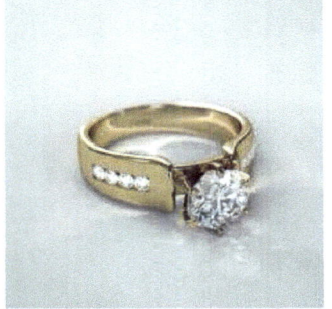

Channel Set Engagement Ring
Starting from $1,580

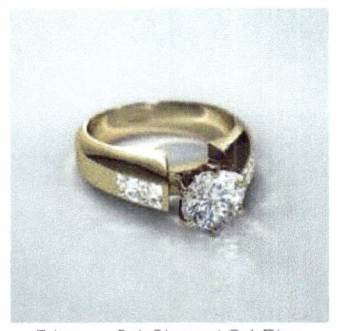

Princess Cut Channel Set Ring
Starting from $1,780

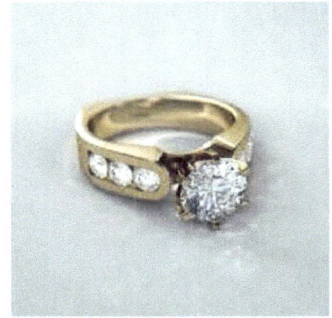

Traditional Round Cut Ring
Starting from $1,800

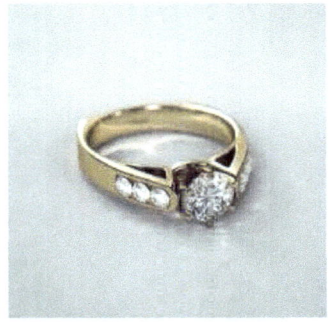

Classic Round Diamond Ring
Starting from $1,510

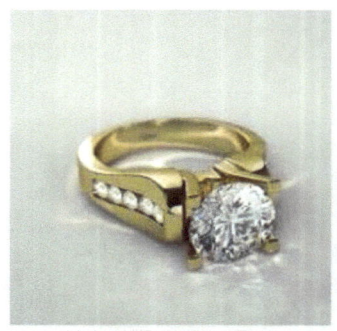

Majestic Sidestone Ring
Starting from $1,860

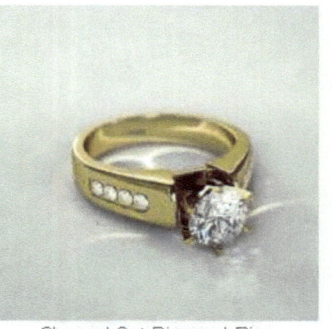

Channel Set Diamond Ring
Starting from $1,580

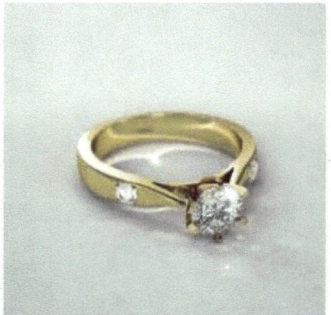

Bezel Set Diamond Ring
Starting from $1,190

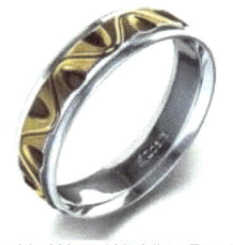

Double Wave Wedding Band
Starting from $560

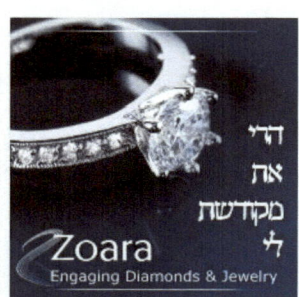

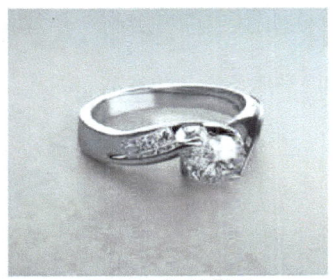

Princess Swirl Ring
Starting from $1,570

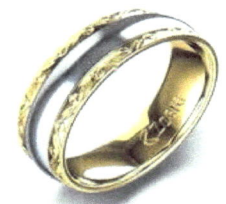

Engraved Two Tone Wedding Band
Starting from $560

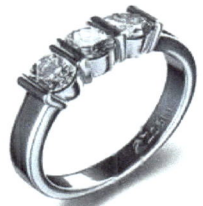

Three Stone Diamond Ring
Starting from $1,200

POPULAR

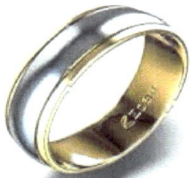

Polished Two Tone Wedding Band
Starting from $610

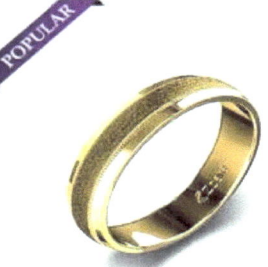

Florentine Milgrain Wedding Band
Starting from $650

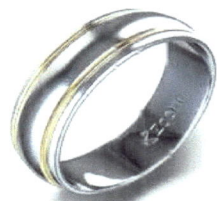

Dual Two Tone Wedding Band
Starting from $680

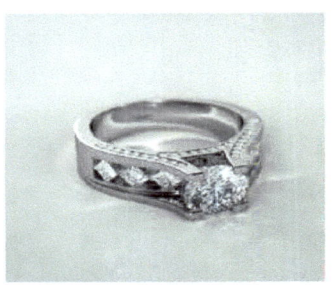

Princess Sidestone Ring
Starting from $3,270

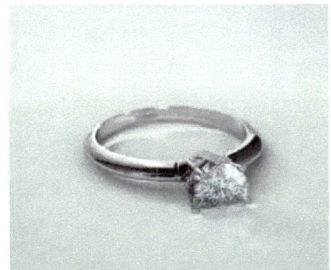

Heart Shaped Diamond Ring
Starting from $675

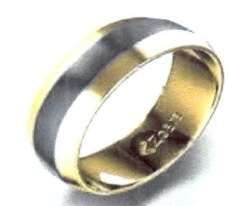

Traditional Two Tone Wedding Band
Starting from $615

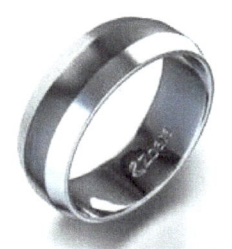

Beveled Edge Wedding Band
Starting from $605

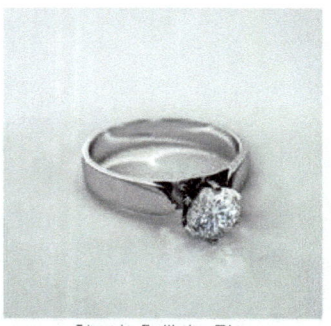

Classic Solitaire Ring
Starting from $760

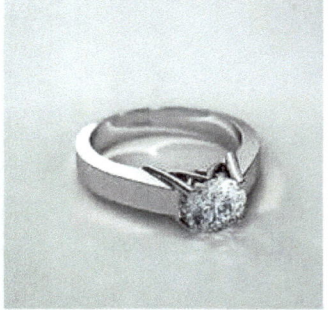

Woven Trellis Ring
Starting from $930

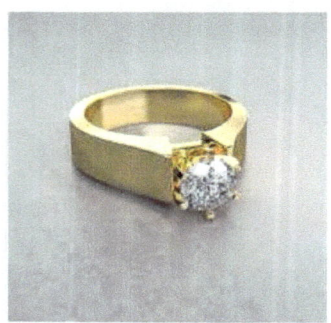

Bold Tapered Solitaire Ring
Starting from $1,310

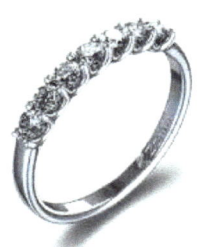

Round Cut 3/8 ctw Diamond Ring
Starting from $935

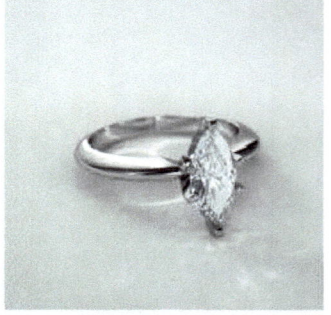

Marquise Diamond Ring
Starting from $675

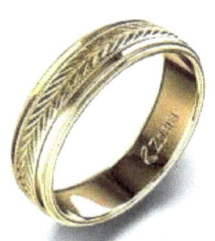

Engraved Laurel Wedding Band
Starting from $650

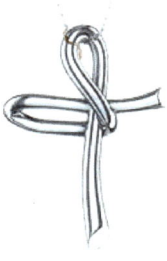

Hoop Designed Cross Pendant
Starting from $330

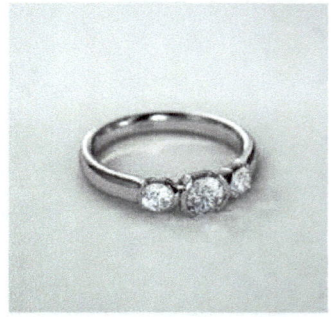

Half Bezel Set Three Stone Diamond
Ring
Starting from $1,300

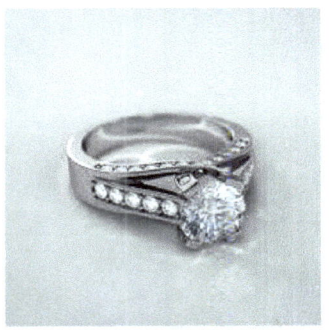

Bead Set Round Diamond Ring
Starting from $1,570

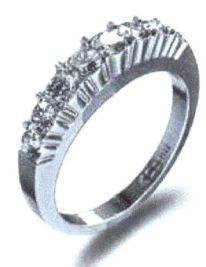

Matching Shared Prong 3/4 ctw
Diamond Ring
Starting from $1,720

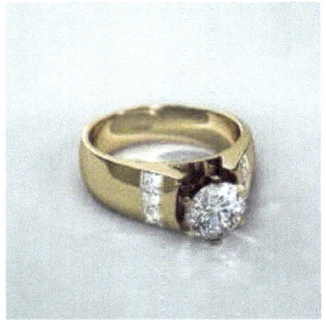

Princess Cut Sidestone Ring
Starting from $1,650

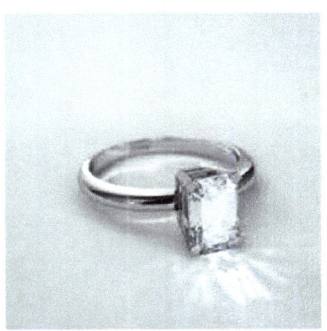

Emerald Cut Ring
Starting from $580

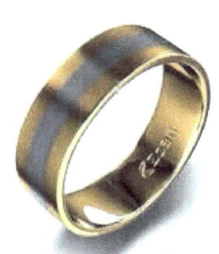

Flat Edged Two Tone Wedding Band
Starting from $730

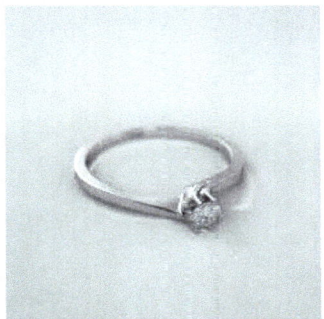

Six Prong Round Diamond Ring
Starting from $720

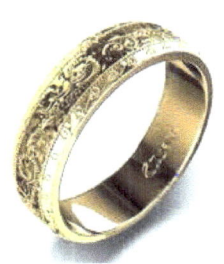

Hand Engraved Wedding Band
Starting from $1,250

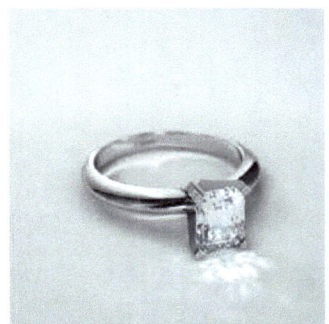

Emerald Cut Diamond Ring
Starting from $700

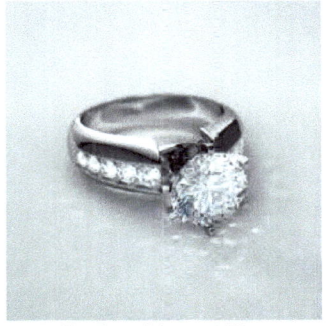

Timeless Diamond Ring
Starting from $2,030

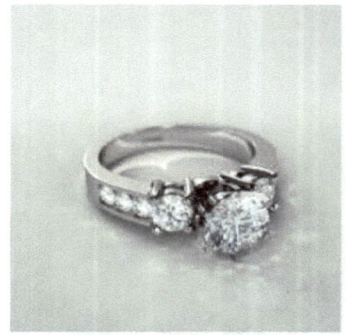

Romantic Diamond Ring
Starting from $2,490

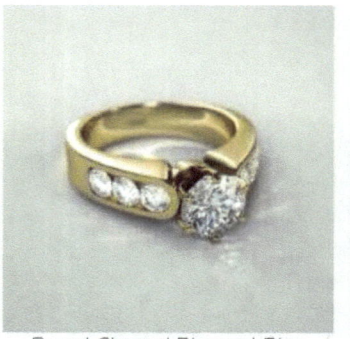

Round Channel Diamond Ring
Starting from $2,590

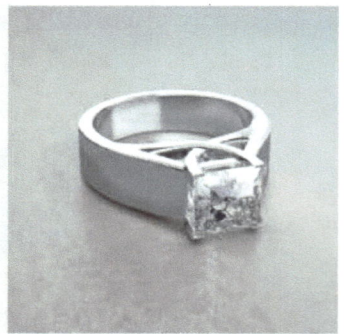

Princess Cut Diamond Ring
Starting from $825

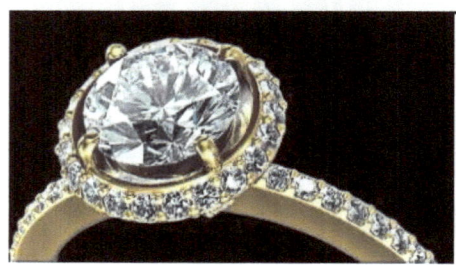

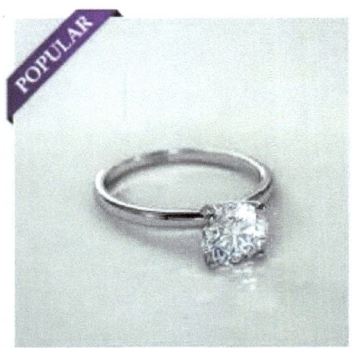

Timeless Four-Prong Round Solitaire
Engagement Ring
Starting from $325

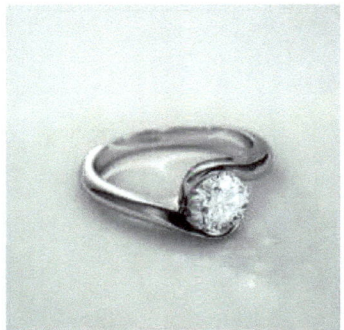

Half Bezel Diamond Engagement
Ring
Starting from $545

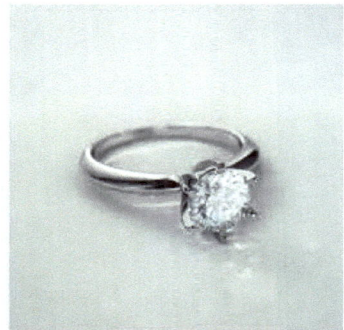

Timelessly Radiant Engagement Ring
Starting from $185

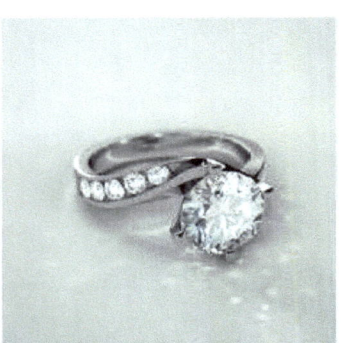

Elegant Twist Diamond Engagement
Ring
Starting from $960

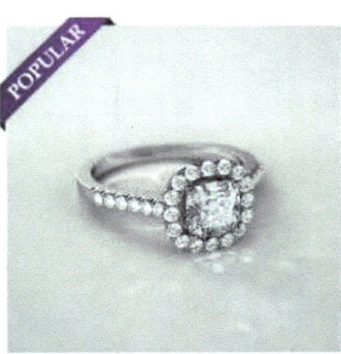

Stunning Cushion Cut Diamond Ring
Starting from $1,440

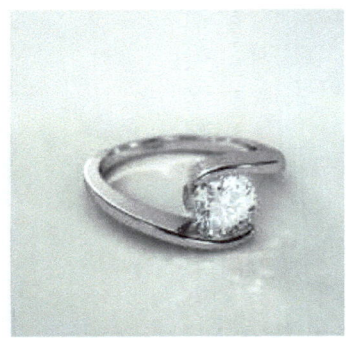

Swirl Bezel Set Diamond Ring
Starting from $475

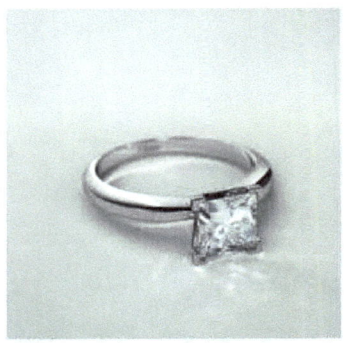

V-Prong Princess Cut Engagement
Ring
Starting from $300

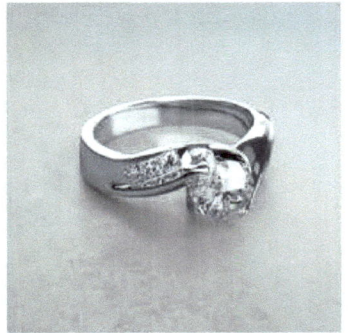

Princess Cut Diamond Engagement
Ring
Starting from $1,670

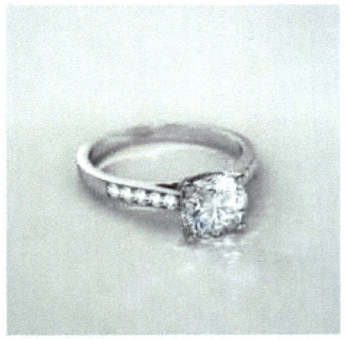

Classic Diamond Engagement Ring
Starting from $730

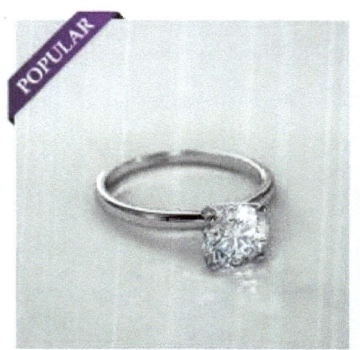

Timeless Four-Prong Round Solitaire
Engagement Ring
Starting from $325

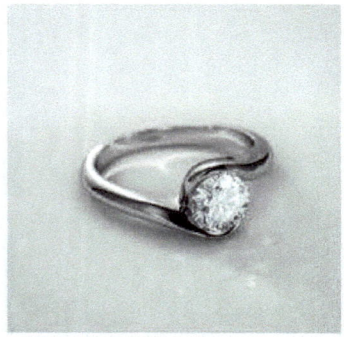

Half Bezel Diamond Engagement
Ring
Starting from $545

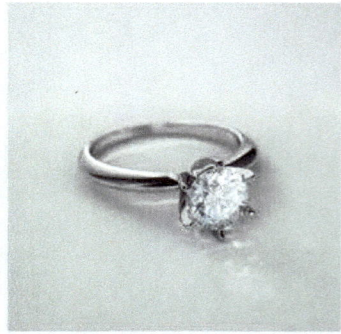

Timelessly Radiant Engagement Ring
Starting from $185

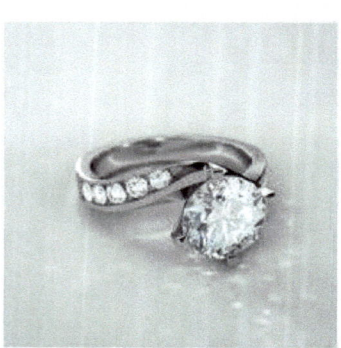

Elegant Twist Diamond Engagement
Ring
Starting from $960

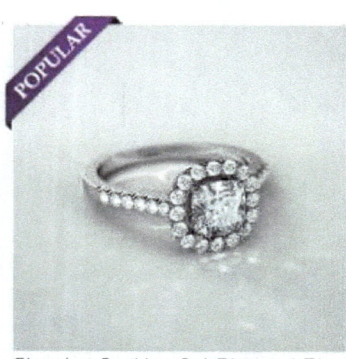

Stunning Cushion Cut Diamond Ring
Starting from $1,440

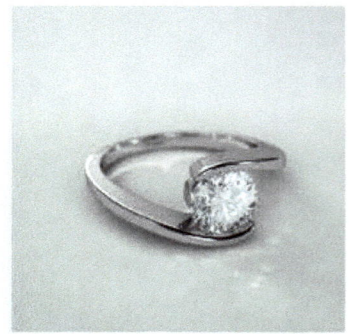

Swirl Bezel Set Diamond Ring
Starting from $475

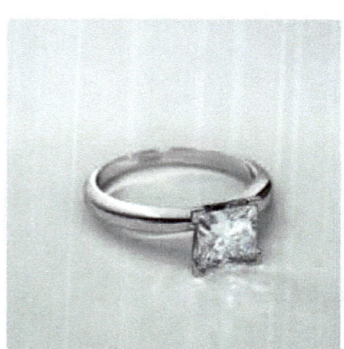

V-Prong Princess Cut Engagement
Ring
Starting from $300

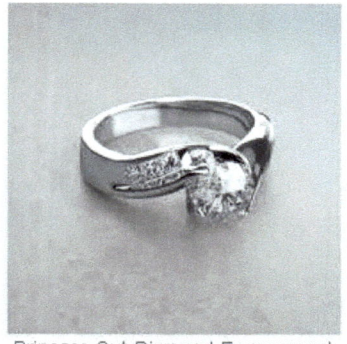

Princess Cut Diamond Engagement
Ring
Starting from $1,670

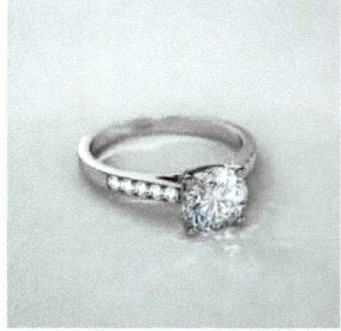

Classic Diamond Engagement Ring
Starting from $730

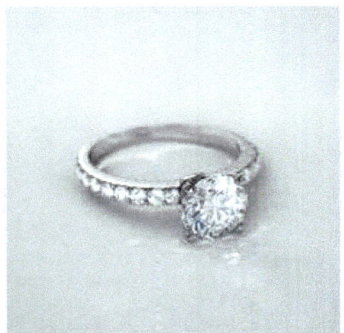

Pave Sidestone Engagement Ring
Starting from $1,130

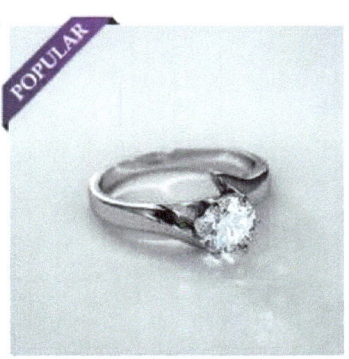

Six Prong Round Diamond
Engagement Ring
Starting from $445

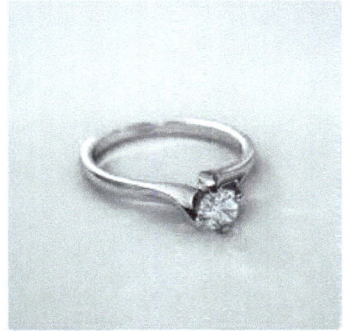

Prong Swirl Diamond Engagement
Ring
Starting from $360

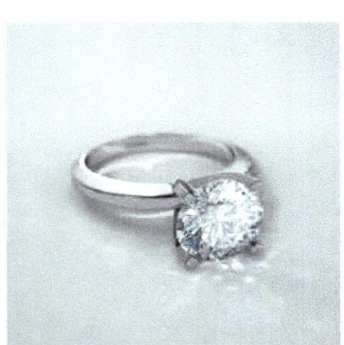

Four Prong Round Cut Diamond
Ring
Starting from $185

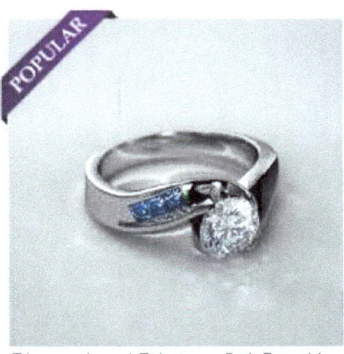

Diamond and Princess-Cut Sapphire
Engagement Ring
Starting from $1,170

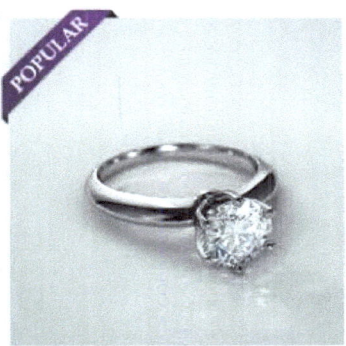

Classic Venus Diamond Engagement
Ring
Starting from $415

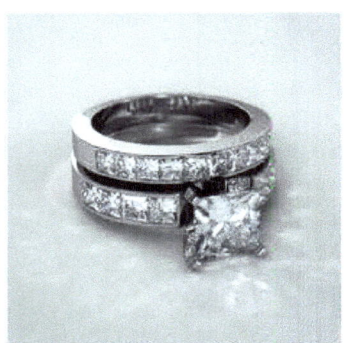

Princess Cut Diamond Wedding Set
Starting from $3,980

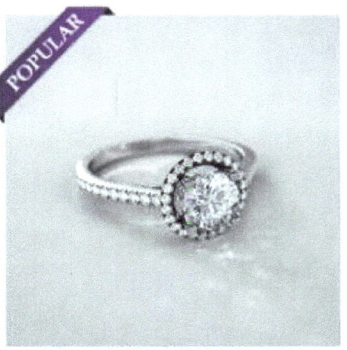

Elegant Halo-Style Diamond
Engagement Ring
Starting from $1,200

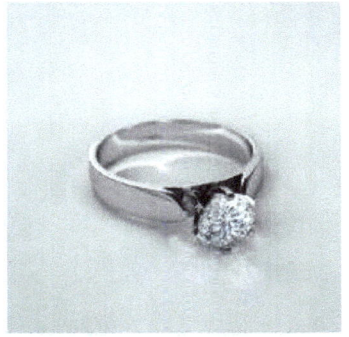

Delicate Tapered Solitaire Ring
Starting from $415

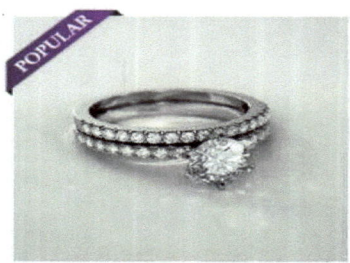

Sidestone Diamond Ring Wedding
Set
Starting from $1,750

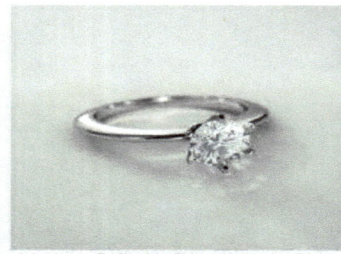

Modern Solitaire Engagement Ring
Starting from $430

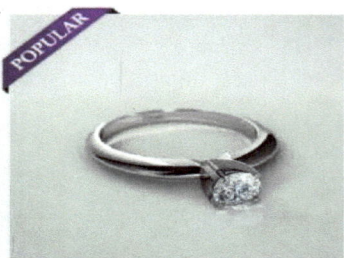

Traditional Round Cut Diamond Ring
Starting from $185

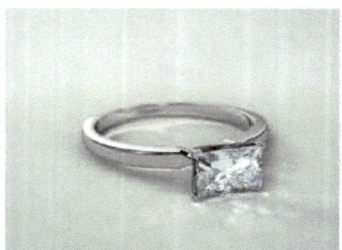

Classic Princess-Cut Diamond
Engagement Ring
Starting from $380

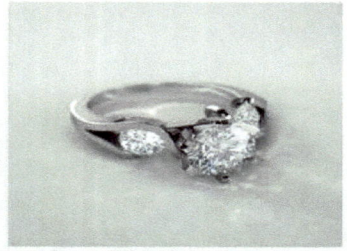

Half Bezel Floral Swirl Diamond Ring
Starting from $1,770

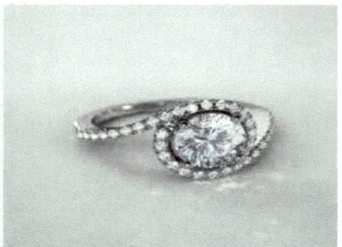

Pave Swirl Diamond Side Stone Ring
Starting from $1,400

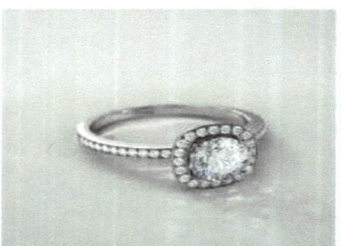

Pave Set Halo Diamond Engagement
Ring
Starting from $1,240

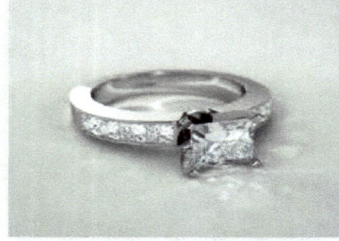

Classic Princess Cut Diamond Ring
Starting from $2,350

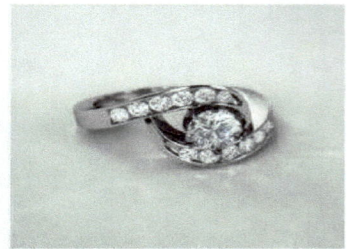

Cleopatra Prong Set Diamond Ring
Starting from $1,900

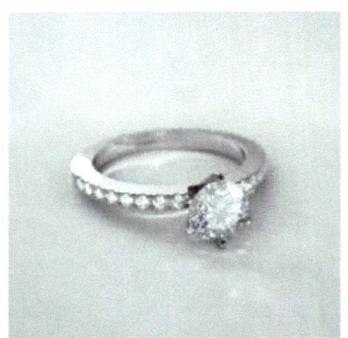
Sidestone Diamond Ring
Starting from $800

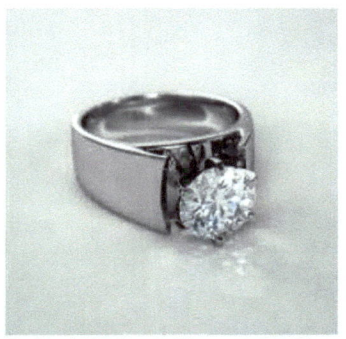
Refined Six Prong Engagement Ring
Starting from $925

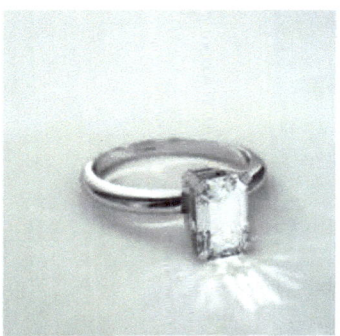
Delicate Emerald Cut Diamond Engagement Ring
Starting from $255

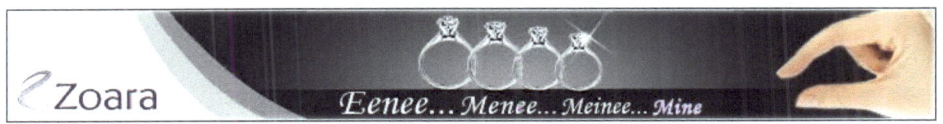

Customers Reviews

Men's Star of David Signet Ring in 14k Yellow Gold
4.5
2 customers reviews average
Ratings Details

Add New Product Review
4/5
Really Unique
I just got this for my husband on the 40th anniversary of his Bar Mitzvah. The ring is really beautiful and definitely not your average gift. The price was pretty decent and ordering it on Zoara was literally painless. We are both very happy with it.
Author: Natalie.L
5/5
Made a Great Gift
Just wanted to say that my father really likes this ring. My family gave it to him for his birthday and he wears it everyday now. The ring is itself looks great on him - its pretty thick and the Star of David is really noticeable. My father says the quality of the metal is excellent, so i'll take his word for it :)
Thanks!
Author: Jenna Marks

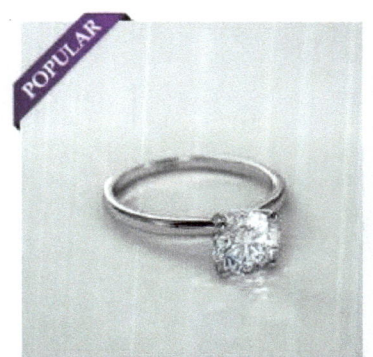

Timeless Four-Prong Round Solitaire
Engagement Ring
Starting from $325

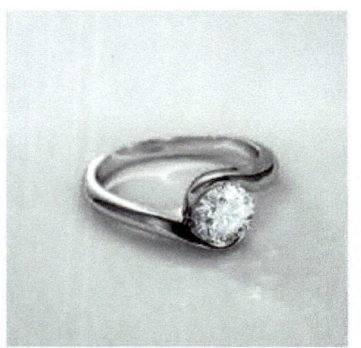

Half Bezel Diamond Engagement
Ring
Starting from $545

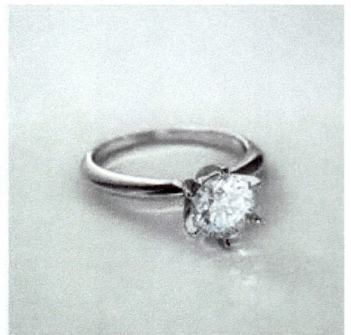

Timelessly Radiant Engagement Ring
Starting from $185

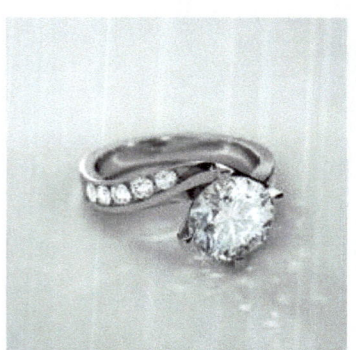

Elegant Twist Diamond Engagement
Ring
Starting from $960

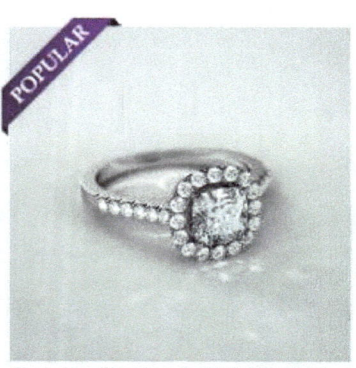

Stunning Cushion Cut Diamond Ring
Starting from $1,440

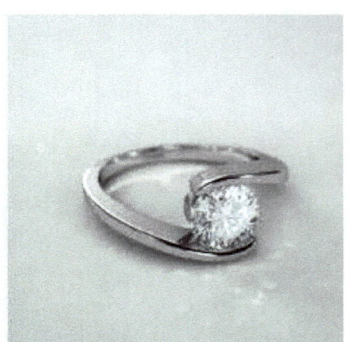

Swirl Bezel Set Diamond Ring
Starting from $475

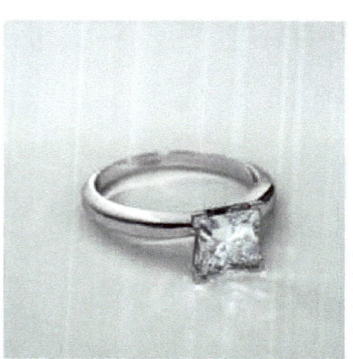

V-Prong Princess Cut Engagement
Ring
Starting from $300

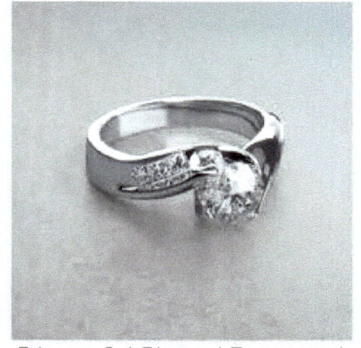

Princess Cut Diamond Engagement
Ring
Starting from $1,670

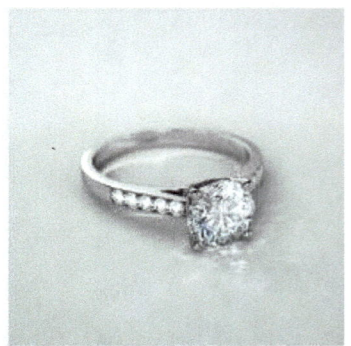

Classic Diamond Engagement Ring
Starting from $730

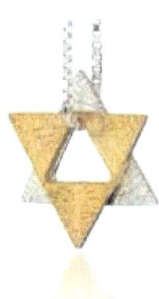

Two Tone Star of David Pendant
with Gold Plating and Silver
Starting from $90

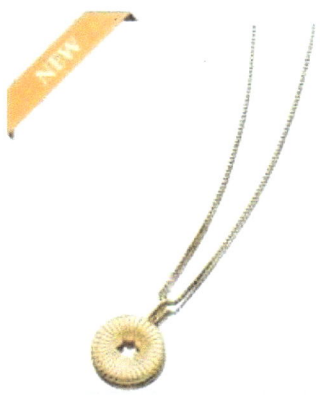

Shell Necklace with Star of David
Starting from $80

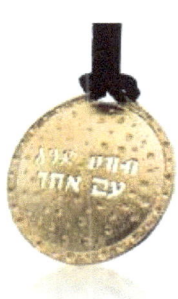

Inscribed Pendant with Hebrew and
Amharic in 24k Gold Plating
Starting from $210

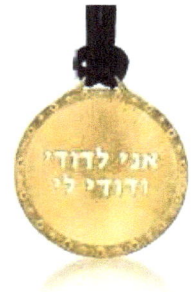

Hebrew Engraved Pendant with
Biblical Verse n 24k Gold Plating
Starting from $220

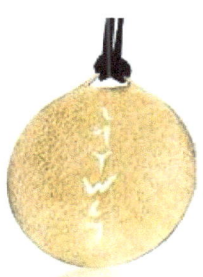

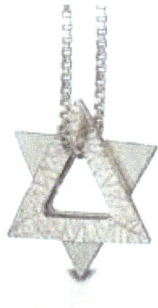

'Jerusalem' Pendant in 24k Plated
Gold with Gezer Alphabet
Starting from $255

Silver Star of David Pendant with
Triangular Design
Starting from $90

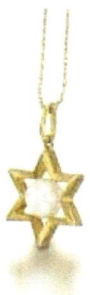

Star of David Pendant with Pearl
Center in Plated Gold
Starting from $125

Textured Star of David Pendant in
24k Gold
Starting from $105

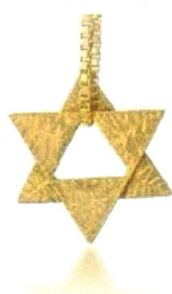

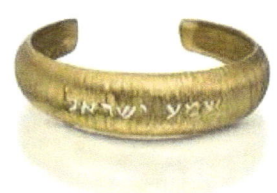

Star of David Plated in 24k Gold with
Triangular Design
Starting from $90

Cuff in 24k Plated Gold with Hebrew
Inscription 'Shema Israel'
Starting from $345

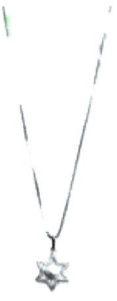

Silver Star of David Pendant with
Fresh Water Pearl
Starting from $100

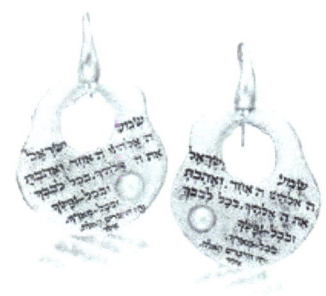

Shema Yisrael Earrings with
Freshwater Pearl
Starting from $150

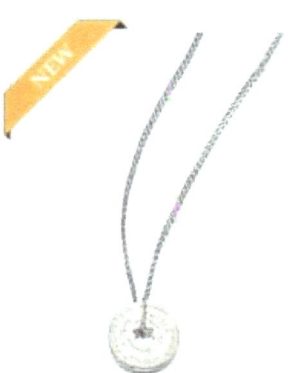

Engraved Jerusalem Necklace
Starting from $80

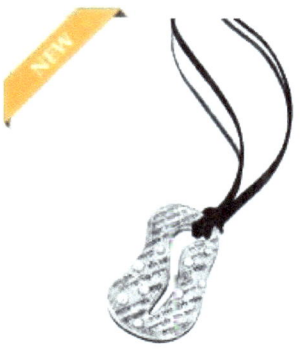
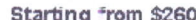

Eshet Chayil Pendant with
Freshwater Pearls
Starting from $260

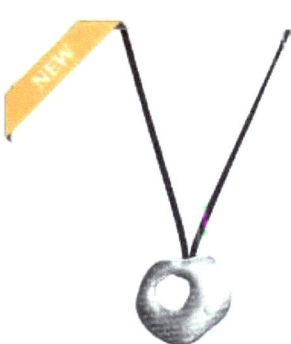

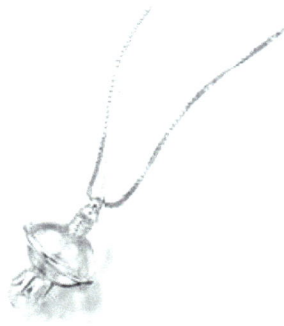

Shema Yisrael Pendant with
Freshwater Pearl
Starting from $200

Pomegranate Pendant with
Freshwater Pearl in Sterling Silver
Starting from $105

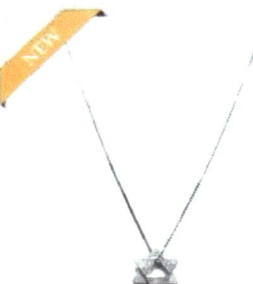

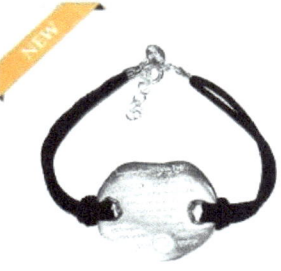

Star of David Pendant with
Interlocking Triangles in Sterling
Silver
Starting from $90

Shema Yisrael Bracelet with
Freshwater Pearl in Sterling Silver
Starting from $150

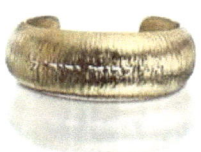

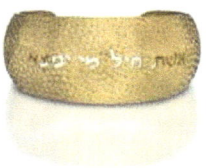

Gold Plated Cuff with Biblical Verse
in Hebrew
Starting from $310

24k Plated Gold Cuff with Hebrew
Inscription 'A Woman of Valor'
Starting from $300

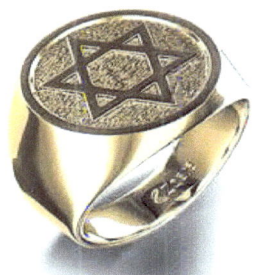

Men's Star of David Signet Ring
Starting from $780

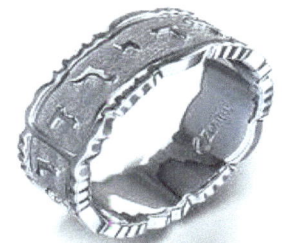

"I Am My Beloved" Hebrew Ring
Starting from $895

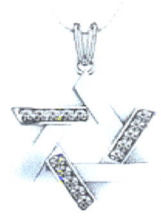

1/8 ctw Star of David Round
Diamond Studded Pendant
Starting from $725

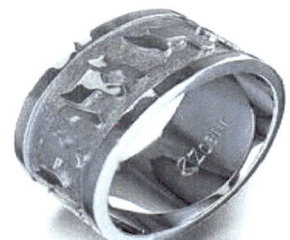

I Am My Beloved Wedding Ring
Starting from $790

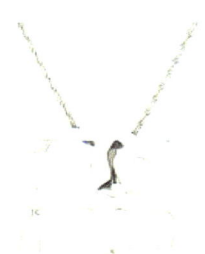

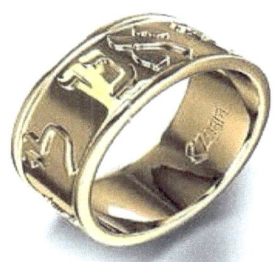

Hebrew "Love" Pendant
Starting from $315

Hebrew Inscribed Women's Wedding
Ring
Starting from $655

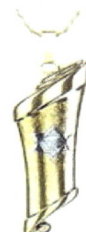

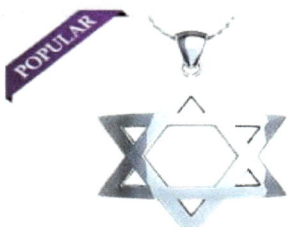

Star of David Mezuzah Scroll
Pendant in Two Tone Gold
Starting from $330

Curved Star of David Pendant
Starting from $290

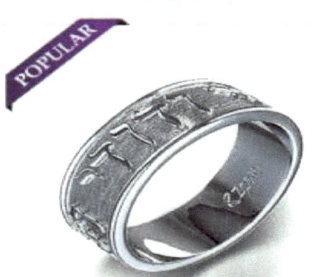

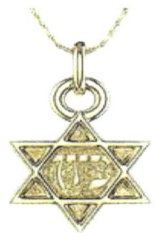

"Ani Ledodi" Hebrew Ring
Starting from $605

"Tzion" Star of David Pendant
Starting from $140

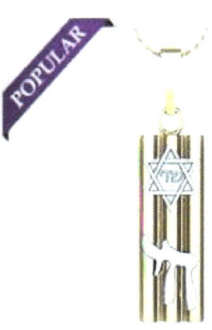

Chai and Star of David Mezuzah
Pendant
Starting from $270

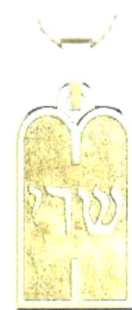

Ten Commandments Pendant in 14k
Yellow
Starting from $350

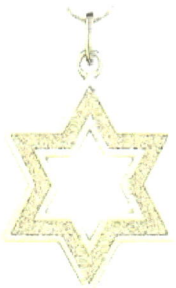

Double Cut-Out Star of David
Pendant
Starting from $160

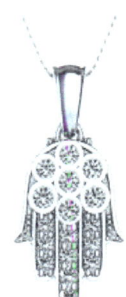

1/4 ctw Bezel Set Hamsa Pendant
Starting from $985

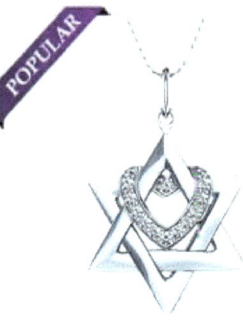

1/10 ctw Heart and Diamond
Studded Star of David Pendant
Starting from $570

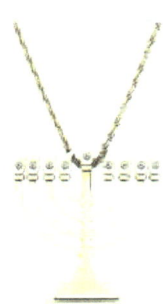

Diamond Studded Menorah Pendant
Starting from $375

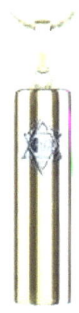

Mezuzah Pendant with Star of David
in Two Tone Gold
Starting from $190

Antique Style Menorah Pendant
Starting from $170

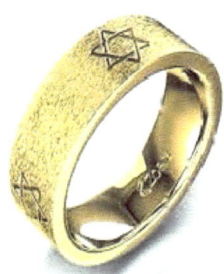

Textured Star of David Wedding Ring
Starting from $845

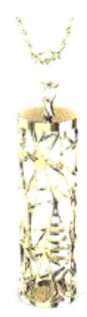

Cut-Out Designed Mezuzah Pendant
Starting from $360

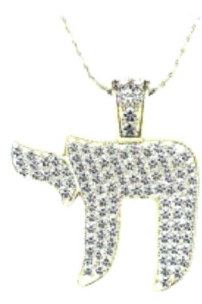

3/4 ctw Diamond Chai Pendant
Starting from $2,170

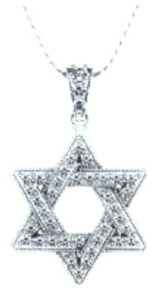

3/8 ctw Diamond Studded Star of
David Pendant
Starting from $1,320

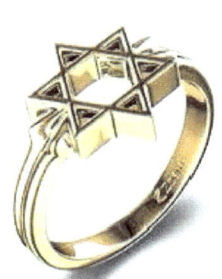

Decorated Star of David Ring
Starting from $290

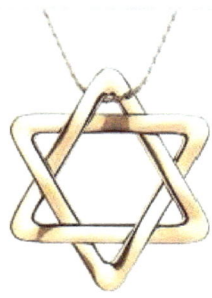

Criss-Cross Star of David Pendant
Starting from $275

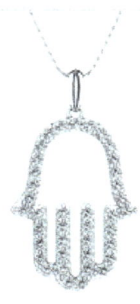

3/8 ctw Diamond Encrusted Hamsa
Pendant
Starting from $1,170

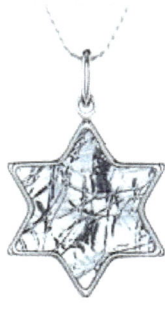

Textured Star of David Pendant
Starting from $305

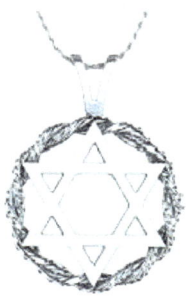

Distinctive Star of David Pendant
Starting from $285

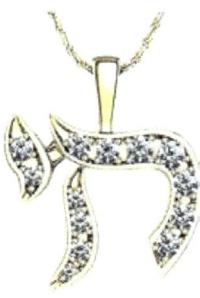

Elvis Presley Inspired Chai Pendant
Starting from $1,040

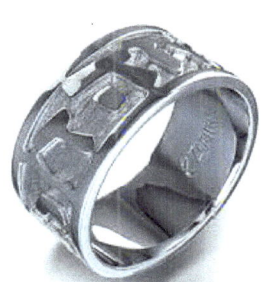

This is My Beloved Wedding Ring
Starting from $905

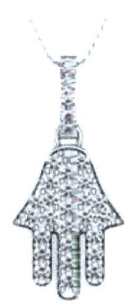

1/6 ctw Diamond Hamsa Pendant
Starting from $750

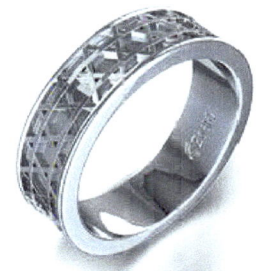

Star of David Wedding Ring in Gold
Starting from $540

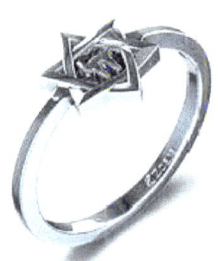

Star of David "Chai" Ring
Starting from $360

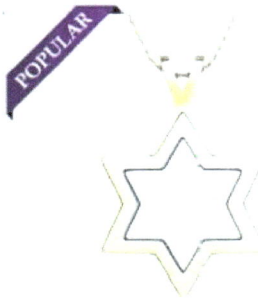

Two Tone Star of David Pendant
Starting from $315

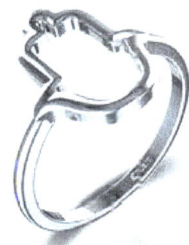

Hamsa Ring
Starting from $260

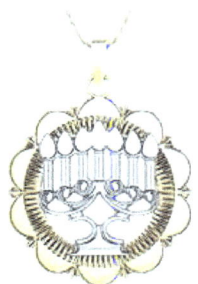

Decorated Menorah Pendant in Two Tone Gold
Starting from $255

1 1/4 ctw Diamond Star of David Pendant
Starting from $2,610

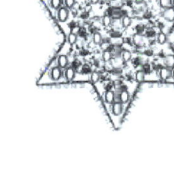

1/6 ctw Designer Star of David Diamond Pendant
Starting from $465

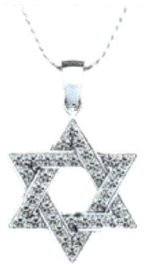

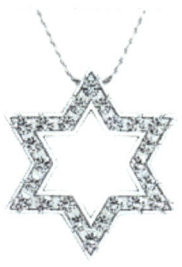

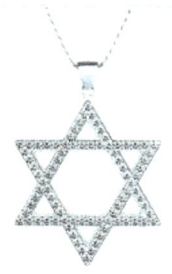

2/3 ctw Classic Diamond Star of
David Pendant
Starting from $1,900

3/8 ctw Cut Out Star of David
Diamond Pendant
Starting from $1,190

9/10 ctw Channel Set Diamond Star
of David Pendant
Starting from $2,890

www.ingramcontent.com/pod-product-compliance
Lightning Source LLC
Chambersburg PA
CBHW050403180526
45159CB00005B/2133